finding home
Rhys
Campbell

finding home

Copyright © 2025 Rhys Campbell

DARK THIRTY POETRY PUBLISHING

ISBN: 978-1-0685766-5-2

Campbell, Rhys
First edition

Artwork by Rhys Campbell
Illustrated by Elijah Bean

DTPP36

DARK THIRTY POETRY PUBLISHING

Dedicated to Rhion Butcher
1998-2024

Finding Home is a poetic journey through the labyrinth of self-discovery and healing. Through raw and reflective verses, this collection dives into the depths of loss, exploring the aching void of grief and the slow, poignant process of acceptance. Each poem paints the struggle of finding one's way back to wholeness, capturing moments of despair, resilience, and the unexpected beauty that arises from brokenness.

As Rhys navigates memories and dreams, the pages become a roadmap for anyone who has ever felt lost, charting a path toward self-reclamation. In finding pieces of themselves scattered by loss, the speaker gradually rebuilds, learning that sometimes "home" isn't a place but a feeling we carry within. Tender, evocative, and deeply relatable, Finding Home reminds us all that we are our own compass and that, even in darkness, we can find a way to the light.

Contents

Trickle 1

Vīrya 3

The River Runs Red 4

Seek 7

The Unlimited Possibilities of Time and Space 8

Awake 10

Heartbeat 12

Spill 13

Blue and White 14

Memories Dissipate 16

Amser/Aimsir featuring Casey-Jade Campbell 17

Vigour 20

Interpretation 22

Protection 23

Renovate 25

Silence 28

Apples featuring Kellan J Blakeway 29

The Delay 31

Vomit 33

Frozen 34

Radio 36

Around Every Corner featuring Bethan Keogh 38

One Day at a Time 39

Worth 41

Cast Out 42

Splatter 43

Somewhat Comfortable 45

Sleeping Well 46

To Be Free   48
Journey   49
Surrender   51
Grief   52
Fingerprints   54
Shades featuring adam Shove   56
The Sound   57
Crowded   59
If They Loved You, They Would Stop   60
The Loneliness of Infinite Space   63
Tests of the Tides featuring Ella Aranyani   65
Set Free featuring Georgia Griffiths   68
Chasing   71
Celerity   72
What does it feel like?   74
To Save Your Life   75
Shadows   76

Trickle

As consciousness trickles down the stream
Letting go of fragile self-esteem
Where the complexity of simplicity
Teaches us authenticity

Listening to the gentle whispers of the night
And the chirping of the morning light
We witness the source in this sound
We witness the spiral in the profound
Where tentative heartbeats are still and pure
Where ancient tradition will eternally endure

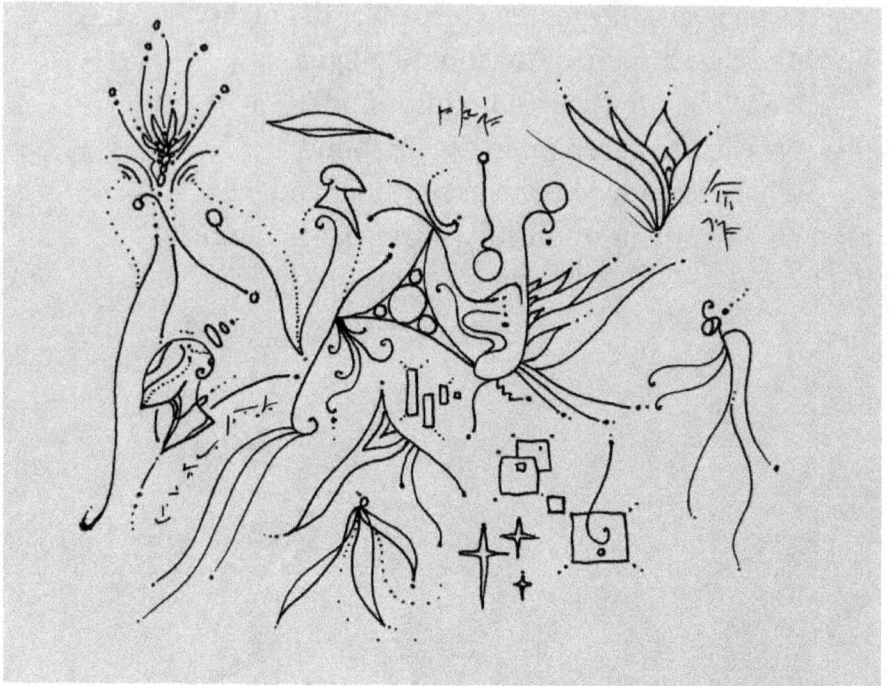

Vīrya

Instead of hunting release
In philosophy and thought
Or forever arguing
Ideologies we've wrought
Lets re-approach
With a new lens

Creativity releases
Stagnation that lies
Beneath layers
However it appears
Because believe me I've
Intellectualised on repeat

Freedom is in our grasp
When Samsara pours out
You'll be screaming "at last"
Through whatever medium
You choose

We can heal burrowed pain
Without dialectic disdain
And you know it to be true
Nirodhah followed through art
The path to a cohesive you

The River Runs Red

As each blurred day adds a layer to the pit in my
stomach
The loss of hope becomes greater and greater
The world watches as we point with well trimmed
nails
When the avoidance is what causes us to fail

The rhetoric already presents itself as redundant
When the ambush has remained constant
For the opposition to grow abundant
It's like we've lost the culture of the ancients
And now the children's facial expressions are vacant
Where the child's gaze of the world has become a
secret

It's fundamental
It's Important
To realise this is gross and pungent
So let's present incumbent
Live free of judgement
But exceptions can be made to this rule
For those that lack morality
For those that leave a sour taste in the mouths of most

What if we tuned into the ambience of nature
We'd be radiant and not wait till later
To love and be loved is the answer
When it feels like there's nothing left to save

The war slaves are brainwashed and obedient
But they've missed the key ingredient
In order to hold ourselves as valiant
And with this attitude we are resilient
Because we can be pure and brilliant
When we don't turn a blind eye to atrocities
When we speak up about doing wrongs

After all we're the same under the skin
So set back and look past that malicious grin
Because we're only now learning to define sin
As we take each day as some form of win
When life doesn't do what it says on the tin

Seek

We're all looking to feel safe and free
To be ourselves in our true glory
To be ourselves and be respected
But some loosely define this space
Crossing them without consent
It's nothing less than theft

It is critical to listen, to pay attention
To the cues that may be uncertain
So just live your life respectfully
With transparency
Wholeheartedly

It's important to inquire, to seek an understanding
Before we enter this masquerade we call existence
To protect yourself and others from needless pain

To respect a friend and their emotions
Is giving love and holding devotion
When we're doing the best we can
And even if this opens to conflict
At least we spoke and listened
Showing acknowledgement
Without the need for avoidance
'Cause that gets you nowhere

The Unlimited Possibilities of Time and Space

Time is the grand navigator
When you are the bold explorer
Reaching the furthest depths of potential
When letting go of the traditional

Reality is measured by observation
It could depend on glee and elation
Or it could be the steady beat of rumination
Or even the dragged out weight
That comes with illumination

Time has a steady beat
A delightful rhythm
Together they harmonise
And this will repeat
Each time the clock completes it's cycle

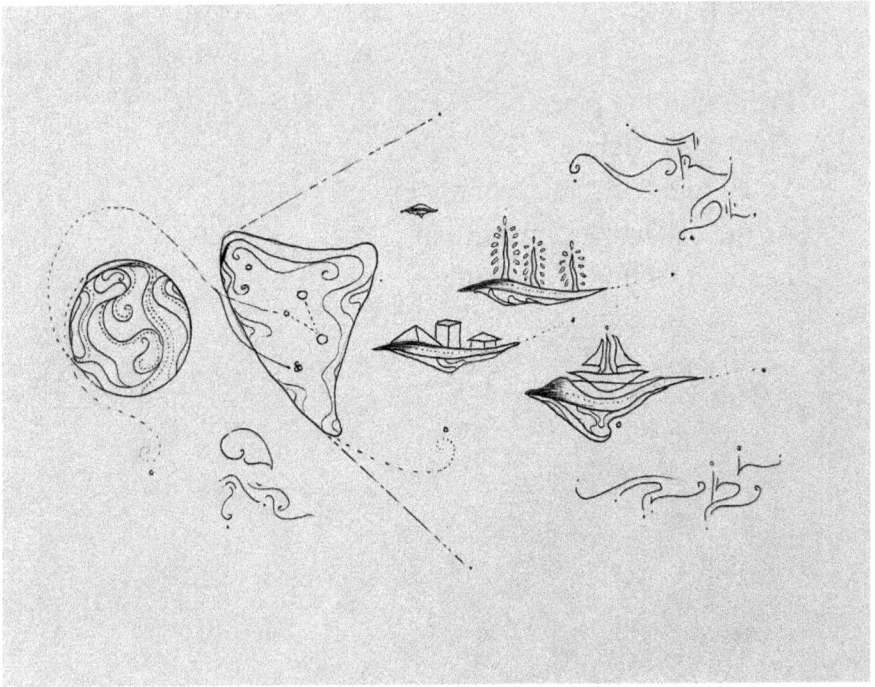

Awake

I'm losing perception
When this feeling heightens
I'm trading sanity for this reality
Saying goodbye to the person I used to be
In this very moment
I feel free

I've found my place
This is my lifeline
So I'll feel the scratch of my breath
As the sea comes crashing in
I submit to this awakening

Heartbeat

As this new feeling was found
It was the birth of sound
When atoms spawned
Greeting the beyond
I felt connected to the ground

Admiration was present
The colours fluorescent
Perspiration and illumination
Heartbeats rise
Feeling alive
I think I've arrived

Spill

I know of things I'll never speak
I want to spill, I am so weak
It's buried deep inside
Cause I swore to secrecy
This weight will one day bury me

Those with faith in me
Were never good to me
In the afterlife, I'll be free

In this life I'm holding high morals
But influence pulls me away like coral
Society is the venom that leaked everywhere
With new eyes, my hearts in my throat
Now witness the sea of tranquility as a dare
Take off the layers, take off that coat
Get ready to set sail, jump on the boat

Blue and White

One brick awaits
The heavy-footed lies
Two lives were taken
In front of the blue and white

It breaks my heart to witness
The brightly coloured night
The thumping sound of helicopters
And the desperate cry of a child

It's hard to fathom security
In the place where they died
But it hurts more to know
That the superheroes
Disguised their lies

Are we really surprised?
After all we've been through
They've always been civilized
It's only the white and blue

Memories Dissipate

The moon will turn its face
In time, another half will fade
We develop a reliance on our loved ones' grace
And it's so easy to be left with a bitter taste
Believing the imprint was a waste

Dwell and be honest
Otherwise, you'll regret it when you want it
It's so easy to be complacent
When you've become compliant
To the lingering black noise

Pressure builds to the surface
When the reminder of mortality emerges dissident
And the sun doesn't set at all
When faced with one's innocence
In cold and rough skin

A lingering silhouette
That's no longer filled with regret
Anguish and torment may come out to play
But love was always here to stay
When our memories have faded away

Amser/Aimsir featuring Casey-Jade Campbell

The haunting time was 22:22
I couldn't escape it and every time, I was ambushed by you.
It was the shadows in the kitchen hanging over my head,
The sound of laughter just right before bed.
The disgust comes and goes of your false pretence.
What was once just a feeling now has evidence.
How I wish there was no sound and that you were just a mime.
Asking myself would I, if I could, turn back the hands of time.
It's full of vibrance, nature's hue,
It can heal the cracks in our souls and renew our views.
The changing of weather and leaves
Can calm minds and make our hearts believe.
After all of the chaos, I'm just trying to find the best in me.
Taking a step back, allowing times tick to make me feel free
From the chains that you once had around us,
Acting as a reminder that everything will someday pass
Teaching us to hold worth in the things that will last.

Breathe it in and let the remedial powers of nature begin.

Vigour

I look at you and witness your pupils grow bigger
In these moments I let my past be a trigger
Maybe I misread, or perhaps I didn't listen
Now your absence makes my want for you thicken
The smell of your perfume and the taste of liquor
But I don't want to chase, I don't want to bicker

A part of me is empty and a part of me is full
A part of me has everything and a part of me's a fool
Yet I make my way even when I'm a tool
You'll have to excuse, I don't make the rules

Interpretation

As humans
We possess the ability to interpret
But does that block our carnal nature
To understand and acknowledge
What our fellow humans are trying to portray?

Responsible behaviour could end
In feelings of betrayal
And actions intended to hurt another
Could end in comforting feelings
Now isn't that odd?

What may appear frustrating for you
Might be one's relaxation
Another's anger state
May present itself as calm
How are we to know
What another bag of flesh of bones is feeling?

Let's take a gaze to the animal world
Where we witness survival
McGregor like brawls
Yet in some parts
It's as if they understood Bob Marley's message.

Protection

Protecting oneself is a cycle you're learning to break
To be emotionally available is one thing
To be romantically available is harder to navigate
Because even when painting your face the right way
You're still left with
Emotional imprints that cause dismay
It'll be right one day
They'll take you as you are with your internal strife
Once you've come to terms and learned to do right
You'll hold hands and walk through life
But the cycle is so vicious
It's hard to break free
So just know it'll be fine
When it's meant to be

Renovate

The price I have to pay is
I've got something to say
I feel contaminated and underestimated
Especially engulfed by this heretic-driven narrative

The poet's consciousness has engulfed me
I no longer correlate ugliness and despair
Seeking art as therapy
As a method for reform
As a method to repair

Seeking out beauty in all of its forms
Appreciating the fabric even if it is torn

The line between pleasure and pain is blurred
The evil within burrows deep and plants its seed
It was forgotten until it bloomed
It flourished
And here it is in its purest form

In darkness it found its shape
Nothing more than a mistake
But nobody could tell you why
You've averted progress
In this masquerade
So pick your poison
And put it on show

Embrace your lows
Find a different tone
When you moan and groan
And sit on your high throne

Hold your sins close and atone
The evil within won't stay
Pave your own way
It's the price you have to pay

Silence

It's crystal clear that you have departed
Feeling alone and far from where it started
You were gone far too soon
And now I sit in this empty room
With no answers but so many questions
Not knowing if I am to learn a lesson
In this tragedy
Because you were like family

I've acknowledged the celestial light
Chasing you and holding you tight
Now that you're free and at peace

Even though the pain may never leave
Many have come together to embrace
The memories and love that weaves
Us all back together
Because you will last forever

I'll carry you with me
And I'll stick it out
Until the very end
Where we meet again

Apples featuring Kellan J Blakeway

Crisp temptation hangs
In bitter tangs
Destitute, soured
Appreciated only by clutching wooden fangs
Insentient until springtime
When blossom softens branched pangs
Releasing far from its captor
Into the wrong hands
Might Eve take a bite
To claim God's spite
Of fruit forbidden in this land?
When it was withered
We took away its leaves
Along with the apples
On this very tree
We could've let it decompose
But benevolence truly knows
The value in bountiful infinity
When the reaction was visceral
There's more than this peripheral
So take it as metaphor or literal
When the apple falls far away from the tree

The Delay

When you pause in the rhythm
Of the eternal dance
You receive a chance
To embrace a hidden trance
Where shadows dance and whispers ring
Where you don't feel a hornet's sting
An enigma stuck in the mask of time
A place that can never be called "mine"
A place where fast and slow intertwine

Vomit

Therapy is like vomiting
A release of pent-up pain
A purging of emotions
A cleansing of the brain

Frozen

Stuck
Like this feeling will last forever
A strung-out process
That feels like laying in a bed of nails
Whilst expressing the details
Of past experiences
Step by step we confront demons
Knowing this has a purpose
A reason

In a world that's turned to stone,
We may find we're all alone,
With jumbled thoughts and broken dreams,
When we're torn at the seams.
Unable to find our way back home

I collect those with contrasting minds
Each of them is a unique find

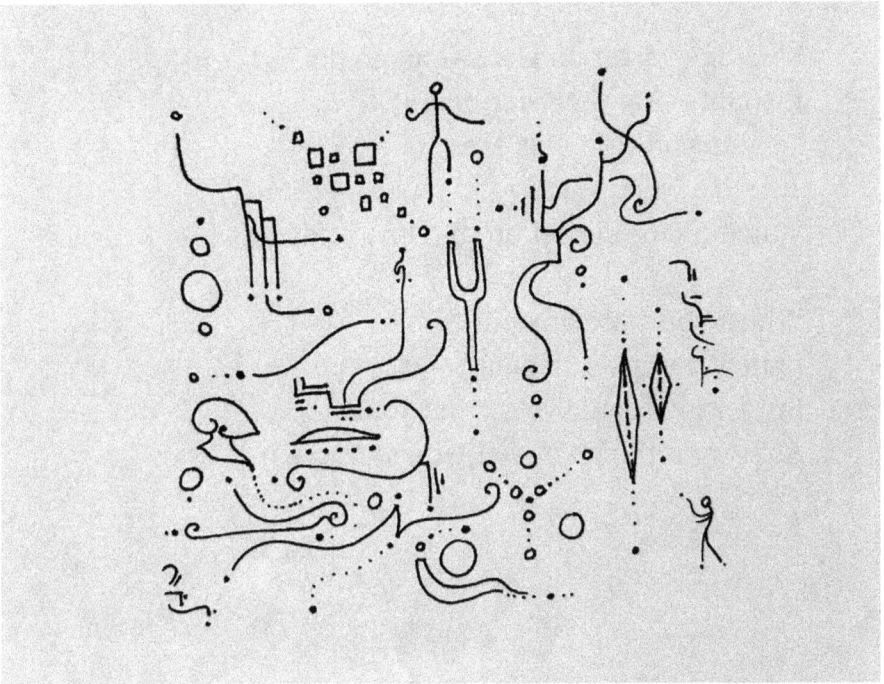

Radio

He turned off his radio to give me support
As the realisation hit as hard as it possibly could
Knowing if I could turn back time
I would
To make sure you were okay

Knowing what you were going to do
I would've sat there for hours
To help you rest your eyes
Just like when we used to sit
Watching the sunset on that tiny bridge

Whilst you were anxious
I knew that pain so well
I just wish I could've carried yours too
After everything you helped me through

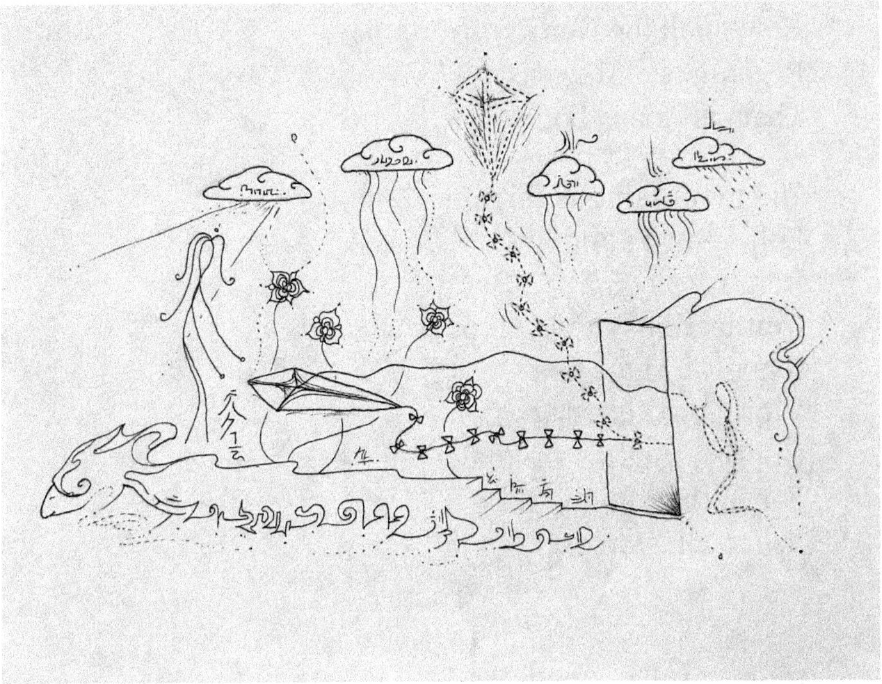

Around Every Corner featuring Bethan Keogh

With humble hearts we explore
The unknown land around every corner
And whilst doing this
We come to see
How small the world truly can be
Regardless of the seas
That part many bodies

The mountainous terrain
Full of highs and lows
Remind us of
Connections made all over
Since we share the
World we know
Cherish the ties we make
For in this tiny world
We're all awake

One Day at a Time

This world is concealed
When we distract ourselves
With rusty thoughts
With disorder

When the sun slowly rises
It provides a new colour palette
To fill up the sky
As the time passes by
We learn we are just fine

With each breath we take
The world continues to move on
And just like the rising sun
We embrace change
As we go along

One day at a time
We face each challenge
With strength and courage
We find our balance
In silence

Constantly rushing to the end
Our worries are always fed
In the present moment
Our worries are shed
In acceptance

Worth

When shadows dance on the walls
The light shines even brighter
And whispers elevate
In this fervent spark
Tracing natural marks
We dance in the dark
We found as time stood still
Darkness began falling
Away from us
And in this moment
We found our worth

Cast Out

I keep looking at the other side
With solitary absence
Collapsing
Who I used to be
Now I can't remember my last dream
Yet I know I ripped the seams
Trying to swallow reason
I lost the exterior I was impervious to
The tower destroyed
Left in rubble
Fog covering remains
Gone are the beggars and saints
But I'll make a new home without sight
In both worlds I'll taste paradise

Splatter

Pride lays out reactions
Dread finds solutions
Gripping on to sustained breath
Knowing I've lost it too many times
I've made it this far
And each backward step taken
Wraps itself in filth

Knowing I can do better
I falter as I pick a side
Struggling to find wrong or right
Each moment a test
As I do my fucking best

Sustaining benevolence
In the hope that nobody
Opens the same doors
Because I've met sorrow

I over-analyse my steps
My mistakes are thorough
But at the end of the day
I know I'll meet tomorrow

44

Somewhat Comfortable

As we lay on the floor
Relaxed and in touch
With every part of our true nature
A reminder that I've found this too much
But now we found in this moment
A new form of rush

When being transparent
Knowing our hearts lie in this room
With pieces missing
Scattered in other places
Wishing to resume
Where we left off

At least we found stillness
When thoughts swirl
Like a hurricane
A moment of quiet
Escaping this mental riot

Sleeping Well

A moment transposed
Anatomy reforms
Renouncing woes
Strengthening bones

One day
We'll see that nobody cared
In quiet everyone stares
With no action or shame
Free of blame

Accountability
Increases durability
And in the end
I'll find transparency

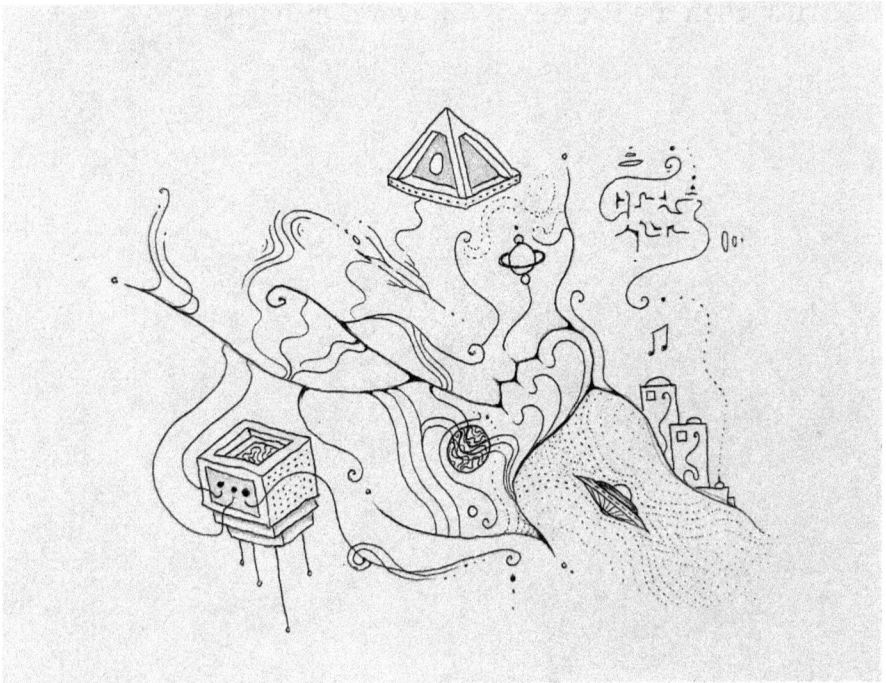

To Be Free

The silhouette of the land on this choppy sea
And the moon glows I truly know
That in this safe space my mind is free
I'll dance until my feet bleed
Because it's my medicine
It's when the stresses of this world truly lessen

Journey

As I walk across the land
I witness the sun and sand
I feel the heart and soul
In everything known

I knew this not too long ago
That there is magic by the water
It's been like this my whole life
Take me away

It was the birth of sound
When the atoms spawned
It all came round

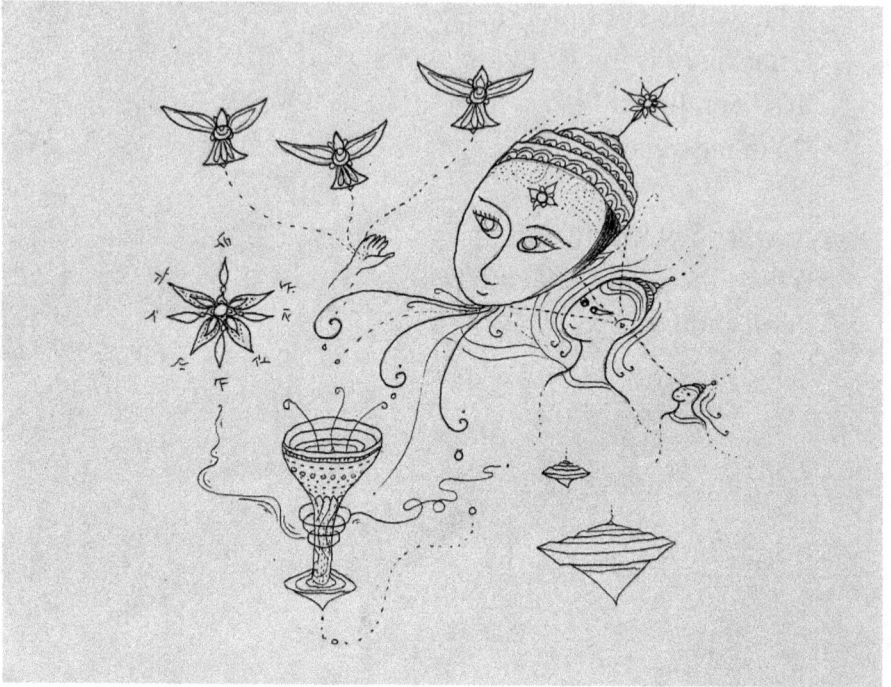

Surrender

In this world we owe them nothing
But truthfully we have to give something
To have this world sustain
And for the love to remain
We won't tolerate games

Everyday we experience new ways
Passing by and accepting new names
Stop and breathe the global repair
And it takes a heart
To heal these scars

In this new world
We understand our place
With compassion and grace
It's our sanity we have to save

Grief

I've stopped counting the days since you left
Because I still feel your breath on the back of my neck
When I sleep and when I wake
You're lost in quantum entanglement
Grounded here yet so far away
All I know is regret
Replaying all of the things I never said

Fingerprints

Given enough to break solid metal
Quietly the moment starts to settle
With a full intake
When the moments right

Curiosity and imagination
Act as a guide to
Explore the universe
Near the surface

I've found a way to explore the sun
Feel it's rays up close
Without having to run
When I'm free of my hopes and dreams

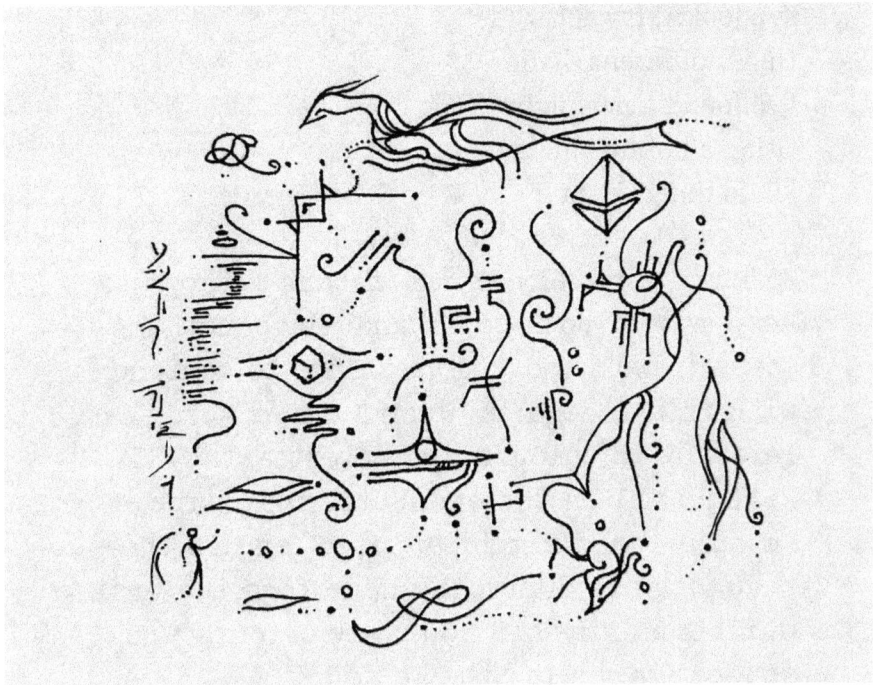

Shades featuring adam Shove

I've been told I'm unhinged
To keep thoughts in
But I've found my outlet
I've let that sink in

I've looked far and wide
Under different shades
I've found a new light
Using all of my might
I'll do things right

So now I actively try different methods to
keep myself both sober and alive, nothing
seems to work, so I have solace to contend
with in a bodega, or when I drive. Words are
relevant to colours and asbestos, they'll
kill us all in the end. Until that happens,
I'm on a long term idea, so as long as the
thoughts are dusty, the haze fogs the brain
while I ask myself how many colours and
shades start with the letter z.

The Sound

In these moments
We learn to love again
I see the pain in your eyes
Knowing I can only listen
And give you the comfort
That you're doing alright

I'm afraid of what happens next
After I've endured too much
And I've lost stillness
With your outstretched hand untouched

Everything is exposed
Foundations and the finished product
Present exactly the same
When we sit together
The same silhouette may not remain
But the love is always here to stay

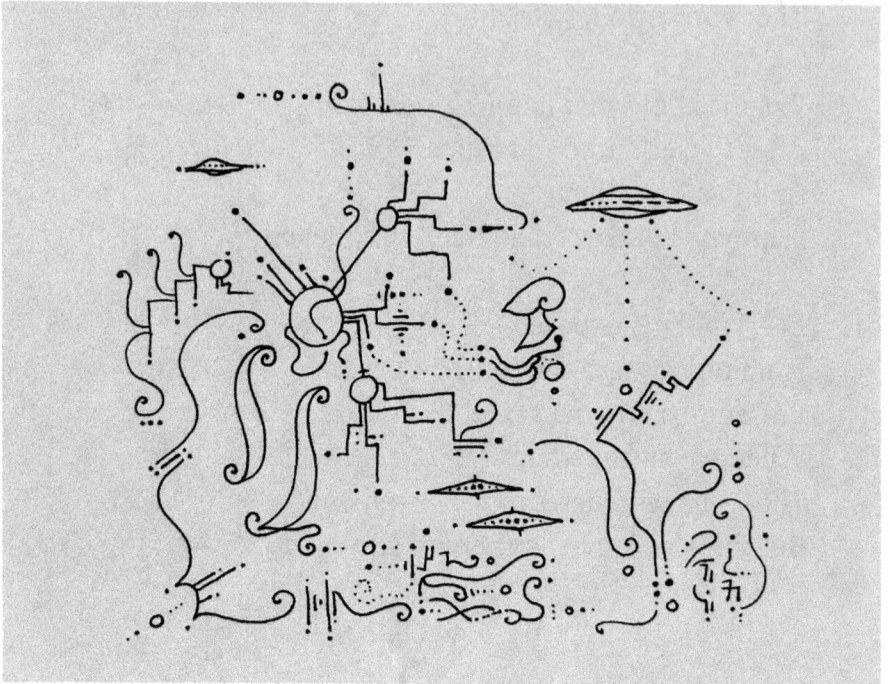

Crowded

In the deepest part of shadows
Whispers dwell
A fractured mind in a brittle shell
Caught in times of deceit

Imitating a world once whole
Fireflies still guide the night
Where a new spark ignites
The truth emerges and feeds the soul

In struggle
Wisdom is gained
The weight of choices
Feel like heavy chains
Yet right where it belongs
The pathways of your heart
Find a path through chaos
Truly unconfined

In the grip of shadows
We learn to see
A way to be free
Facing the light

If They Loved You, They Would Stop

"If they loved you, they would stop" they say
As if it's hold on me could go away
As if the thick void inside could cease
With a whispered praise
With an act of peace

The conflict is rarely seen outside of the mind
The demons lie and keep it confined
In the fog of longing and despair
It's not that I don't love
Sometimes I'm not there
And my heart is being repaired

The heart that loves is still inside
But buried beneath the endless tide
Of craving
Of need
Of shadows that creep
In the moments of stillness
In the deepest of sleeps

"If they loved you..."—the guilt and weight
As if this alone could change my fate
It's myself who will find the cure
A way to heal the scars endured

When darkness could consume me

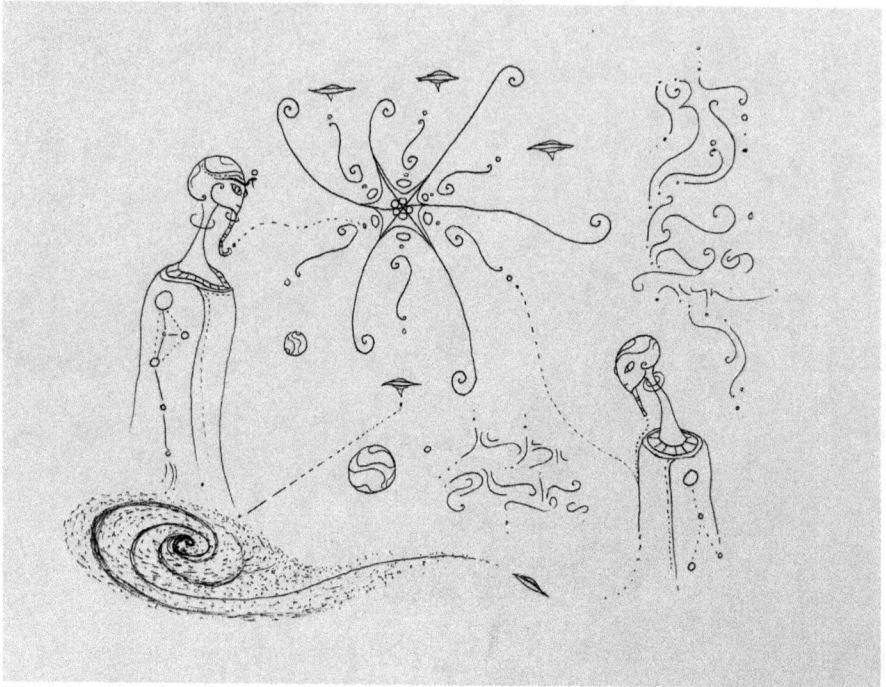

The Loneliness of Infinite Space

I found solace in the deepest of depths
Where a solitary vessel drifts in a vast expanse
Silent waves crash against my embrace
Desolation won't signal the end of this dance
As I sail in the night where shadows creep
Next to memories in the tides calmness sweeps
And it's the warmth I will keep
Ensuring loneliness won't take its toll
As the ocean's rhythm soothes my delicate soul

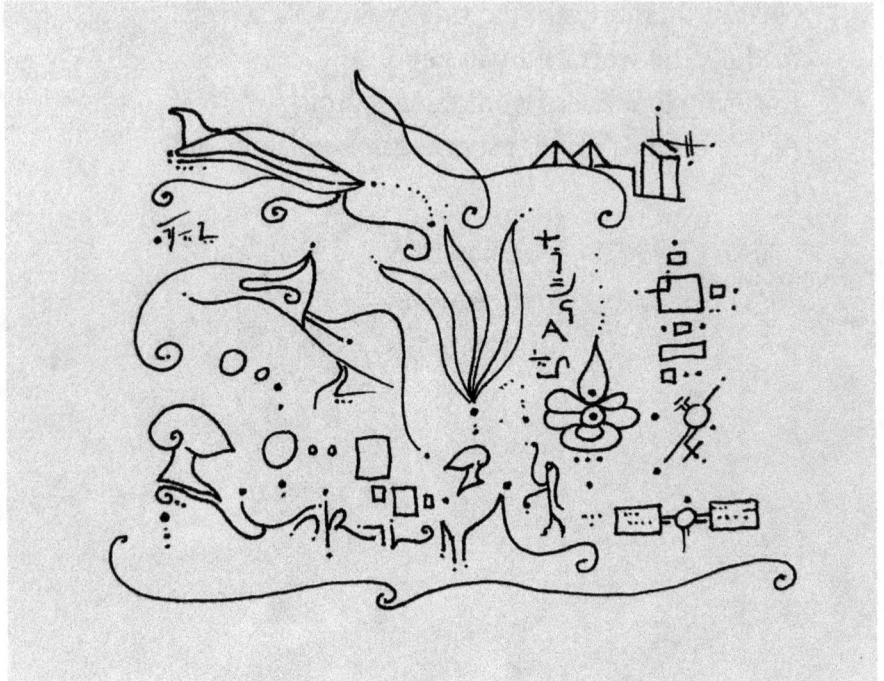

Tests of the Tides featuring Ella Aranyani

old ways to the waves
I drowned in the water and became anew
washed upon the shore
baptised and bruised, yes
but alive once more

dusting off the sand
and the soreness of yesterday
I focus on all that's left of me
and it's ... everything

I thought I was falling apart
but I was coming back together
piece by piece
then I found a letter written by the future me
it came in a bottle washed up by the sea

she told me the ways in which I could be free
so I listened intently
as the whispers of spirit danced around me

and with each passing moment
I began to see it as it was
I wasn't being swallowed by the tides
but thrown into the depths
of who I could be
not a cracked shell
but polished by the very same waves

it was comfortable at the bottom
where it's overwhelmingly busy
where abundance had become rotten
and we sit soaked in misery

no— not for me

I kept the letter
since its words spoke like an ancient song
singing chants of freedom
without the need to chase it
'cause it was there all along

Set Free featuring Georgia Griffiths

You've lost the ache that you used to feel
After you sought a novel way to heal
Your neurons adapted
And spat on the fire
Left your life in a state of satire

You're not the person that I once knew
Filled with desire, love, and lust
From our childhood dreams that are now combust
Now tried and lonesome, just floating dust
We tried and tested ways to heal
Forgetting how to really feel
But you still don't burn the way you should
Or even the way you thought you would
And as I'm stood, waving you off
I hope you still don't pay the cost
I hope your good
And I hope your better
Please don't forget me
And don't forget her

I'll write you notes,
A hundred love letters
I'll tell you you're amazing
And that I need you around
Remind you to take deep breaths
And listen
To the rhythmic sound
Of your heart

Let it pound -

I mean it,
I need you
And I want you around—
I need you, I said
I need you to be safe and sound
So please give yourself a fighting chance
Please snap out of this autopilot trance
You'll laugh again in dreams expanse
You'll dance across the pearly gates
Not wade in sadness
Through the fields of hate
You'll skate to me with open arms
And we'll indulge in life's wondrous charms -
I need you, I said
So please don't give up
I told you
You fill up my empty cup
For I am you
And you are me
And so our minds must now be free
For you to be you
And me to be me

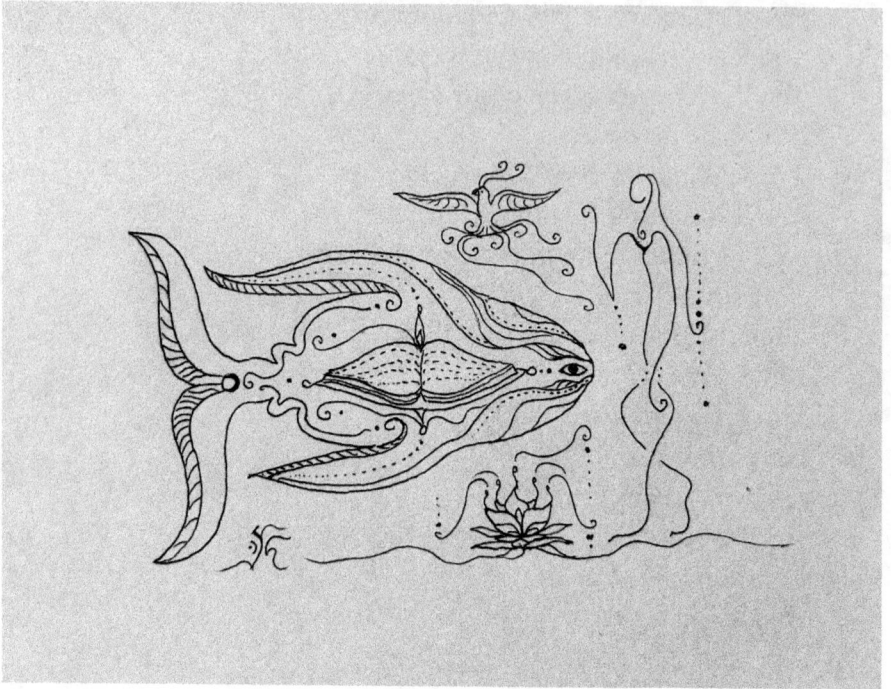

Chasing

I'll spend my life trying to understand
How my mind can't keep up with the unplanned
But we call this living each day
In simplicity we pave a new way
But yet I am willing
To show efficiency
Without latency
In harmony

Celerity

I felt the world liven
Eyes opening for the very first time
Its heartbeat thrummed silence
A rhythm lost
Now found in my own

I saw it as it truly was
Raw beauty wrapped in fragile grace
A tapestry of life
Untethered
Bound only by the stars in space

When the last generation falters
Delivering its final
Trembling blow
The linger of its weary journey
Still whisper secrets we must know

From ashes rise new voices, calling
To mend the wounds, to light the way
A dawn reborn, the world still turning
Awake
Alive
To greet the day

What does it feel like?

Making the earth shake
Breaking what we cannot remake
Disposing of our waste
In the water that we taste

I've been feeling it as of late
The weight of consequence, the twist of fate
The fright, the fight
Trying to make it through the night

What does it feel like to ignore the call
To watch as the balance begins to fall
Are we too late to truly hear
The earth crying out in a voice so clear

It won't be long until we're washed away
Since the sea was always here to stay
What of the lands that cradle our dreams
Devoured by relentless streams

To Save Your Life

You sit across the table
A quiet storm in your eyes
Little did I know
This was your goodbye
You told me you loved me
You said "can I call you tomorrow?"
Yet in reflection
I saw the depths of your sorrow
I want to tell you
I know the way back
I've traced the paths out of despair
The sun still rises
No matter how long the night lingers there
You thought it was too late
That the cracks had spread too far
But I want to scream
You're wrong
To grab your hands
To pull you from the edge
To show you a life beyond this
If I had stayed
I might've saved your life

Shadows

As the light hits the walls
The wounds have been cleansed
As part of this eternal mess
So take a moment to rest

The lines on the walls shiver
A sense of freedom delivers
And you've considered parallels
Because you feel the harmony in symmetry
Witnessing this beautiful imagery

A huge thank you to Adam for consistently providing an exceptional environment for me to express myself freely. Thank you to Bondage Zine, for the republication; and more significantly, to my dear friends and family for their inspiring presence and unwavering support.

About The Author

Rhys Campbell born Bermudian, grew up in and currently resides in Cardiff, in the land of dragons which moulded him to be the person he is today. Self-taught, he started writing for himself at the tender age of 14.

Rhys often conveys his poetry within the verbalised art form that is spoken word. You can find his work on all major streaming platforms usually complemented with ambient instrumentals to further ensure the impact of the message.

@rhysc.ampbell

RELEASED BY DARK THIRTY POETRY

ANTHOLOGY ONE
THIS ISN'T WHY WE'RE HERE
MORTAL BEINGS
POEMS THAT WERE WRITTEN ON TRAINS BUT
WEREN'T WRITTEN ABOUT TRAINS
CLOSING SHIFT DREAMS
DESIRE
ANIMATE
THESEUS AND I
I DON'T HAVE THE WORDS FOR THIS
CONVERSATIONS BETWEEN THE SUN AND THE
MOON
SLUT POP
JADED
I'VE BIRTHED AN IDEA OF YOU
BRUISES
CITY GOTHIC
LONG DIVISION
SAY HER NAME
LUMIN
VESTIGES
FALLING IN LOVE LOST
JUGGERNAUT
STIRRING TO LIFE
FORGOTTEN FRAGMENTS OF TIME
THIS BOOK IS NOT ABOUT JAPAN
BEYOND THE DOORS OF A LAST BREATH
CORPORATE
JANE F*CKING EYRE
THE SNAKE EATS ITSELF
THE MOON AND HER CRATERS
NOCTURNAL
BREWING ANXIETEA
FLAT FRONT
ARE YOU HAVING A GOOD TIME YET?
WORDS TAKE SHAPE

ICARUS ISN'T DEAD
FINDING HOME